Prentice Hall

Biology

Animated Biological Concepts Worksheets

Prentice
Hall

Upper Saddle River, New Jersey
Glenview, Illinois
Needham, Massachusetts

ISBN 0-13-064506-0

10   07 06

Contents

Worksheet	Page	Correlation to *Prentice Hall Biology*

Worksheet 1

Atomic Structure

PART A *Complete the table.*

	DEFINITION	EXAMPLE
Compound	a.	c.
Element	b.	d.

PART B *Match each of the characteristics with the correct subatomic particle or particles by writing a letter or letters on the lines provided.*

1. _____ positively charged

2. _____ orbits the nucleus

3. _____ uncharged or neutral

4. _____ smaller than other particles

5. _____ negatively charged

6. _____ found in the nucleus

a. electron

b. proton

c. neutron

Worksheet 2

Energy Levels and Ionic Bonding

PART A *Define the following on the lines provided.*

1. Ion

_____

_____

_____

2. Chemical bonds

_____

_____

_____

PART B *Answer the following on the lines provided.*

ENERGY LEVEL	NUMBER OF ELECTRONS LEVEL CAN HOLD	NUMBER OF ELECTRONS AT THIS LEVEL IN A CHLORINE ATOM	NUMBER OF ELECTRONS AT THIS LEVEL IN A SODIUM ATOM
First (lowest energy)	a.	d.	g.
Second (higher energy)	b.	e.	h.
Third (highest energy)	c.	f.	i.

1. Complete the table by writing the correct number of electrons in each of the cells.

2. What information in this table would lead you to predict that sodium and chlorine could form an ionic bond? Explain your answer.

_____

_____

_____

_____

Worksheet 3

Covalent Bonding
....

PART A *Complete the diagrams.*

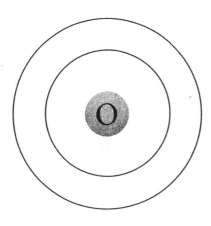
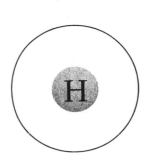

1. Complete the above diagrams of the oxygen and hydrogen atoms by drawing their electrons.

PART B *Answer the following on the lines provided.*

1. Explain how the information in this diagram indicates that an oxygen atom could bond covalently to two hydrogen atoms to form water.

_____

_____

_____

_____

_____

_____

2. Explain the difference between single, double, and triple covalent bonds.

_____

_____

_____

_____

_____

_____

Worksheet 4

Enzymatic Reactions

PART A *Answer the following questions on the lines provided.*

1. What is the function of an enzyme?

_____

2. What type of organic compounds are enzymes?

_____

3. What substance takes part in an enzymatic reaction but is unchanged by the reaction?

_____

4. Sucrase is an enzyme that breaks sucrose down into glucose and fructose. What happens to the chemical bonds in sucrose when it binds to the enzyme sucrase?

_____

5. Many genetic diseases result from the production of enzymes that are not shaped properly. Why could a change in shape cause an enzyme to work poorly or not at all?

_____

_____

PART B *Match each component in the enzymatic reaction below with the name of that component by writing the letter on the line provided. Use each letter only once.*

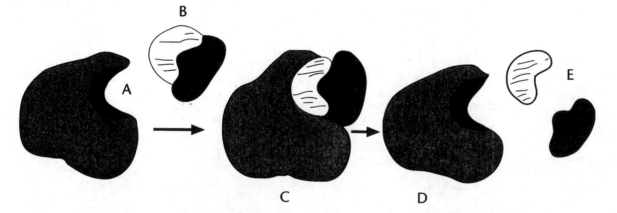

1. _____ enzyme-substrate complex

2. _____ enzyme

3. _____ products

4. _____ active site

5. _____ substrate

Worksheet 5

Diffusion and Osmosis
■ ■

PART A *Define the following terms on the lines provided.*

1. Diffusion

_____

_____

2. Semipermeable membrane

_____

_____

3. Osmosis

_____

_____

PART B *Answer the following.*

1. Complete the table.

TYPE OF SOLUTION:	ISOTONIC	HYPERTONIC	HYPOTONIC
Effect on Cell Placed in Solution:	a.	b.	c.

2. Freshwater protozoans, such as *Paramecia*, must constantly pump out water to keep from bursting. What does this tell you about the solute concentration inside a *Paramecia* compared to the solute concentration of its environment?

_____

_____

_____

3. What would happen if you made the solute concentration outside the *Paramecium* the same as that inside it?

_____

_____

_____

Worksheet 6

Passive and Active Transport

▪ ▪

PART A *Complete the table by writing* Yes *or* No *in each square.*

	ACTIVE TRANSPORT	FACILITATED TRANSPORT	DIFFUSION
1. Requires energy input	a.	b.	c.
2. Moves molecules against their concentration gradients	a.	b.	c.
3. Requires a membrane protein	a.	b.	c.
4. Sodium-potassium pump is an example	a.	b.	c.

PART B *Answer the following questions on the lines provided.*

1. Name a substance that can diffuse across the cell membrane.

_____

2. Name a substance that is too large to diffuse across the cell membrane.

_____

3. What prevents charged molecules from diffusing across the cell membrane?

_____

_____

4. How is facilitated transport similar to simple diffusion?

_____

_____

_____

5. How does facilitated transport differ from diffusion?

_____

_____

_____

6. How is facilitated transport similar to active transport?

_____

_____

_____

7. How does facilitated transport differ from active transport?

_____

_____

_____

_____

8. Briefly describe the action of the sodium-potassium pump.

_____

_____

_____

_____

Worksheet 7

Endocytosis and Exocytosis

PART A *Define the following terms on the lines provided.*

1. Exocytosis

_____

2. Endocytosis

_____

3. Phagocytosis

_____

PART B *Answer the following questions on the lines provided.*

1. Describe how endocytosis and exocytosis are similar.

_____

_____

2. Describe how endocytosis and exocytosis differ.

_____

_____

_____

3. What is a vesicle?

_____

_____

4. The term phagocyte literally means "cell eater." Explain why some white blood cells are called phagocytes.

_____

_____

5. What process is an amoeba using when it engulfs a food particle?

_____

6. What is a lysosome and what is its function?

_____

_____

7. What would you expect to find in exocytotic vesicles?

_____

_____

12 *Animated Biological Concepts*

Worksheet 8

ATP Formation

PART A *Answer the following questions on the lines provided.*

a. _____

b. _____

c. _____

1. Label each part of the ATP molecule above in the spaces provided.

2. What is ATP an abbreviation for?

_____

3. What is the sugar in ATP called?

_____

4. How does ATP differ from ADP?

_____

_____

5. Explain how ATP is like a rechargeable battery.

_____

_____

_____

PART B *In the space provided, draw and label the ATP Cycle. Include the following: ATP, ADP, phosphate, energy required, energy released.*

Animated Biological Concepts **13**

Worksheet 9

Photosynthesis

▪▪

PART A *Answer the following questions on the lines provided.*

1. What is photosynthesis?

_____

_____

_____

_____

2. What molecules, produced by photosynthesis, are used to store energy from the sun?

_____

PART B *Use the diagram of photosynthesis below to answer the following.*

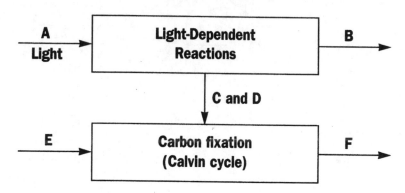

1. Identify the compound each letter represents.

a. _____

b. _____

c. _____

d. _____

e. _____

f. _____

2. How do plants obtain the carbon dioxide they need for photosynthesis?

_____

_____

_____

_____

_____

_____

Worksheet 10

Light-Dependent Reactions

PART A *Match each structure with its function by writing the letter of the structure on the line provided.*

1. _____ Uses the energy released by the flow of hydrogen ions to convert ADP to ATP.

2. _____ Uses light energy to split water.

3. _____ Uses light energy to re-energize electrons.

4. _____ Transfers electrons between light-collecting molecules.

5. _____ Region where hydrogen ions accumulate when water is split.

a. photosystem I

b. photosystem II

c. electron carrier protein

d. ATP synthase

e. thylakoid space (lumen)

PART B *Answer the following questions on the lines provided.*

1. Explain the role of light energy in the light-dependent reactions.

_____

_____

_____

_____

_____

2. Describe the location of photosystems I and II inside the chloroplast.

_____

_____

_____

_____

_____

3. What two high-energy compounds are created by the light-dependent reactions?

_____

_____

_____

_____

_____

Worksheet 11

Calvin Cycle

▪ ▪

PART A *Use the diagram to answer the questions below.*

b. _____

a. _____

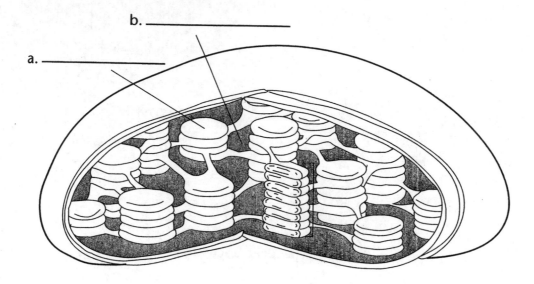

1. What is this organelle called?

_____

2. Label the parts of the organelle in the spaces provided.

3. Circle the name of the part where the Calvin Cycle takes place.

PART B *Complete the description of the Calvin Cycle below by filling in each of the blanks with one of the following: ATP, RuBP, NADPH, or PGA.*

1. The Calvin Cycle begins when one molecule of carbon dioxide is added to each of

three (**a**) _____ molecules to form three 6-carbon molecules. Each of the

6-carbon molecules splits in half to form two 3-carbon molecules of (**b**) _____ .

The cell "spends" molecules of (**c**) _____ and (**d**) _____ to energize the

3-carbon molecules. This forms six molecules of PGAL. One of the newly formed PGAL

molecules leaves the cycle. The remaining five PGAL rearrange into three molecules of

(**e**) _____ . This rearrangement requires the cell to "spend" three more molecules

of (**f**) _____ .

Worksheet 12

Aerobic Respiration

PART A *Complete the table.*

AEROBIC RESPIRATION	
REACTANTS	PRODUCTS
1.	2.

PART B *Match each description with the correct process or processes by writing a letter or letters on the lines provided.*

1. _____ occurs in the cytosol

2. _____ produces pyruvate

3. _____ yields up to 32 ATP molecules

4. _____ produces carbon dioxide

5. _____ occurs in the mitochondria

6. _____ breaks down glucose

7. _____ final stage in aerobic respiration

a. glycolysis

b. electron transport

c. Krebs cycle

Worksheet 13

Glycolysis

■ ■

PART A *Answer the following questions on the lines provided.*

1. What carbon compound is broken down by glycolysis?

_____

2. How many carbon atoms are in this starting compound?

_____

3. What carbon compound is the final product of glycolysis?

_____

4. How many carbon atoms are in this product?

_____

5. What energy-carrying compound is used to start glycolysis?

_____

6. Your cells are carrying out glycolysis right now. Where do they get the raw materials for this process?

_____

PART B *Use the diagram to answer the question below.*

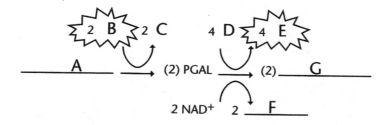

1. Identify the missing compounds in the simplified diagram of glycolysis by filling in the blanks below.

a. _____

b. _____

c. _____

d. _____

e. _____

f. _____

g. _____

Worksheet 14

Krebs Cycle
∎∎∎

PART A *Answer the following questions on the lines provided.*

1. Describe what happens to each of the three carbons in pyruvate during the reactions that precede the Krebs cycle.

    _____

    _____

    _____

2. Name the three different kinds of high-energy compounds created during the Krebs cycle.

    _____

    _____

    _____

3. Describe the formation of citric acid, the first intermediate in the Krebs cycle.

    _____

    _____

    _____

4. What happens to the carbon molecules that are released as citric acid is broken down from a 6-carbon compound to a 4-carbon compound?

    _____

    _____

    _____

5. Why is the Krebs cycle called a cycle?

    _____

    _____

    _____

6. What happens to the high-energy compounds produced by the Krebs cycle?

    _____

    _____

    _____

7. What happens to the carbon dioxide molecules produced during the Krebs cycle?

    _____

    _____

    _____

PART B *Use the diagram to complete the following.*

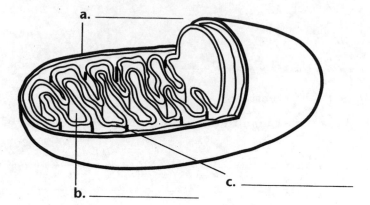

1. What is this organelle called?

_____

2. Label the parts of the organelle in the spaces provided.

3. Circle the name of the part where the Krebs cycle is carried out.

Worksheet 15

Electron Transport Chain

PART A *Answer the following questions on the lines provided.*

1. In what organelle does electron transport take place?

_____

2. What compound is NADH converted to when it transfers high energy electrons to the first electron carrier?

_____

3. Describe the first electron carrier. What is it made of and where is it located?

_____

_____

_____

4. Where does the first electron carrier pump hydrogen ions?

_____

5. How does the amount of energy that electrons have change as they are passed along the electron transport chain from one electron carrier to the next?

_____

_____

6. What is the final electron acceptor at the end of the electron transport chain?

_____

7. Describe how the difference in hydrogen ion concentrations between two areas is used to create ATP.

_____

_____

_____

_____

8. At what point during electron transport is water formed?

_____

_____

_____

_____

Animated Biological Concepts **21**

PART B *Identify each labeled part or area of the diagram of the electron transport chain below.*

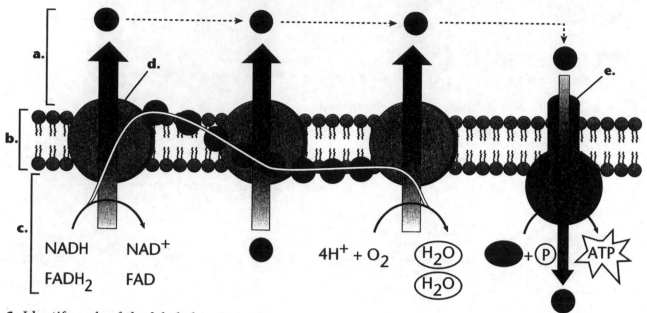

1. Identify each of the labeled parts or areas.

a. _____

b. _____

c. _____

d. _____

e. _____

PART B *Complete the diagram below by drawing the products of meiosis I and meiosis II for this cell.*

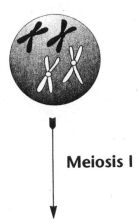

Meiosis I

Meiosis II

Worksheet 18

Animal Cell Meiosis

■ ■

PART A *Match each of the descriptions with the appropriate phase of meiosis by writing the letters on the lines provided.*

1. _____ Homologous chromosomes condense, the nuclear envelope dissolves, and spindle fibers form.

2. _____ Homologous chromosomes are lined up at the center of the cell.

3. _____ Homologous chromosomes are pulled apart and moved to opposite ends of the cell.

4. _____ Cytokinesis occurs, and two haploid daughter cells are formed.

5. _____ Chromosomes of the two haploid cells become attached to spindle fibers.

6. _____ Chromosomes line up in the center of each of the two haploid cells.

7. _____ The attachment between sister chromatids breaks. Each sister chromatid is now considered a daughter chromosome.

8. _____ Each haploid cell completes division, producing a total of four haploid daughter cells.

a. anaphase II

b. prophase II

c. anaphase I

d. prophase I

e. metaphase II

f. telophase II

g. metaphase I

h. telophase I

PART B *Use the diagram to answer the questions below.*

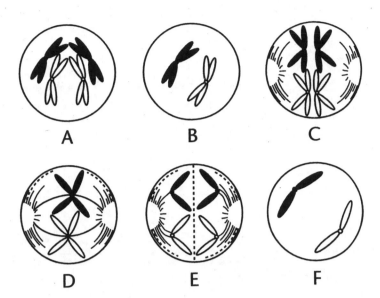

A   B   C

D   E   F

1. Which graphic shows a cell in metaphase I of meiosis? _____

2. Which graphic shows a cell in metaphase II of meiosis? _____

3. Which graphics show diploid cells? _____

4. Which graphics show haploid cells? _____

5. Which graphic shows the final product of meiosis I? _____

6. Which graphic shows the final product of meiosis II? _____

Worksheet 19

Segregation of Chromosomes

PART A *Define the following terms on the lines provided.*

1. Gene

_____

_____

2. Allele

_____

_____

3. Diploid cell

_____

_____

PART B *Answer the following questions on the lines provided.*

1. Explain how homologous chromosomes resemble one another and how they differ.

_____

_____

_____

2. Describe what happens to homologous chromosomes during anaphase I of meiosis.

_____

_____

_____

3. Explain how the behavior of chromosome pairs during meiosis is related to the segregation of alleles.

_____

_____

_____

4. Based on what you know about the segregation of alleles, explain why all egg or sperm cells are not genetically identical.

_____

_____

_____

PART B *Answer the following questions on the lines provided.*

1. What is the first step in DNA replication?

_____

_____

_____

2. What enzyme matches the bases of free nucleotides to the bases on the parent strand?

_____

3. Explain why one DNA strand grows one nucleotide at a time and the other is assembled in short fragments.

_____

_____

_____

_____

4. If the DNA double helix were a twisted ladder, what would the sides of the ladder be made of?

_____

5. What would the rungs of the ladder be made of?

_____

6. Complete the table below.

NUCLEOTIDE BASE	ABBREVIATION	COMPLEMENTARY BASE	
a.	T	e.	
b.	C	f.	
c.	A	g.	
d.	G	h.	

Worksheet 22

Crossing Over

▪ ▪

PART A *Use the diagram of two homologous chromosomes to answer the questions below.*

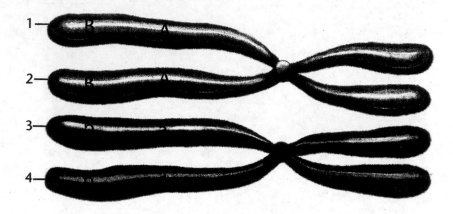

1. What is the number of the sister chromatid to chromatid 1?

_____

2. What is the number of the sister chromatid to chromatid 4?

_____

3. What are the numbers of the two chromatids with which chromatid 2 could exchange alleles by crossing over?

_____

4. During what stage of meiosis does crossing over occur?

_____

PART B *Complete the table by writing one allele combination in each cell.*

Possible Allele Combinations	
WITHOUT CROSSING OVER	**ONLY WITH CROSSING OVER**
a.	c.
b.	d.

Worksheet 23

Human Sex Determination
■ ■

PART A *Complete the table by drawing in the spaces provided.*

	SEX	
	MALE	FEMALE
Draw and label the sex chromosomes.	a.	c.
Draw the types of gametes produced. Show their sex chromosomes.	b.	d.

PART B *Answer the following questions on the lines provided.*

1. How many pairs of autosomes are in a man's liver cells?

_____

2. How many pairs of autosomes are in a woman's liver cells?

_____

3. Which parent's genetic contribution determines the offspring's sex? Explain your answer.

_____

_____

_____

_____

Worksheet 24

Nondisjunction

. . . .

PART A *Use the diagram to answer the question below.*

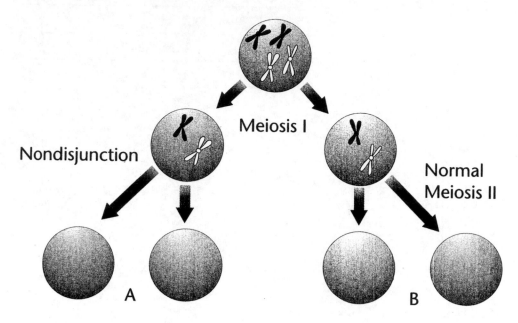

Meiosis I

Nondisjunction

Normal
Meiosis II

A

B

1. Complete the diagram by drawing chromosomes in the gametes.

PART B *Answer the following questions on the lines provided.*

1. What effect does nondisjunction have on the chromosome number of the gametes?

_____

_____

_____

_____

_____

_____

2. Down syndrome, a genetic disorder in humans, results from an extra copy of chromosome 21. Explain how a person could come to have an extra copy of this chromosome.

_____

_____

_____

_____

_____

_____

Worksheet 30

Gene Transfer and Cloning

PART A *Define the following terms on the lines provided.*

1. "Sticky ends"

_____

2. Plasmid

_____

3. DNA ligase

_____

PART B *Answer the following questions on the lines provided.*

1. How is human DNA prepared for use in gene transfer?

_____

_____

_____

2. How is bacterial DNA prepared for use in gene transfer?

_____

_____

_____

3. Explain what happens when bacterial DNA and human DNA that have been cut with the same enzyme are mixed together.

_____

_____

_____

4. Tetracycline is used as a medicine to treat bacterial infections. What allows some bacteria to grow even if tetracycline is present?

_____

_____

_____

5. How do scientists use tetracycline resistance to find the bacteria that contain the gene for human insulin?

_____

_____

_____

Animated Biological Concepts

Worksheet 31

Lytic and Lysogenic Cycles

- -

PART A *The steps in the lytic cycle are shown below. Describe what is happening in each.*

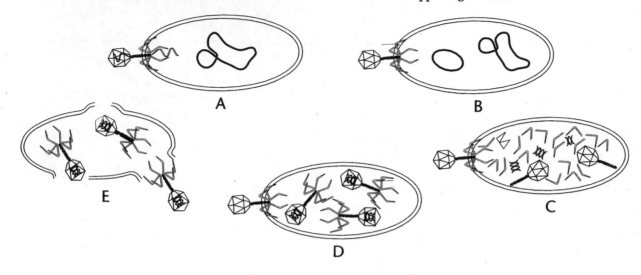

a. _____
_____
_____
_____
_____

b. _____
_____
_____
_____
_____

c. _____
_____
_____
_____
_____
_____

d. _____
_____
_____
_____
_____

e. _____
_____
_____
_____

PART B *Answer the following questions on the lines provided.*

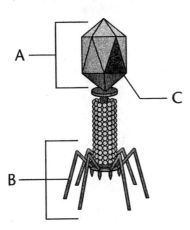

1. Identify the viral nucleic acid in the diagram above.

_____

2. Explain how the lysogenic cycle differs from the lytic cycle.

_____
_____
_____
_____
_____

3. What is a prophage, and during which type of viral replication is it formed?

_____
_____
_____
_____

4. What is a host?

_____
_____
_____
_____

5. Explain how the lytic and lysogenic cycles are linked.

_____
_____
_____
_____

Animated Biological Concepts   **43**

Worksheet 32

Water Transport in Plants

∎∎

PART A *Define the following on the lines provided.*

1. Transpiration

_____

_____

2. Xylem

_____

_____

PART B *Answer the following questions on the lines provided.*

1. How can plants prevent water loss?

_____

_____

2. What vital substance do plants obtain through their pores?

_____

3. What effect does the closing of guard cells have on transpiration?

_____

_____

4. What are a plant's water-carrying vessels called?

_____

5. According to the cohesion-tension theory of water transport, what creates the negative pressure that carries water upward from the roots to leaves?

_____

_____

_____

_____

6. According to the cohesion-tension theory of water transport, what causes water molecules to stick together as they are carried upward from the roots to leaves?

_____

_____

_____

_____

© Pearson Education, Inc.

Worksheet 33

Sugar Movement in Plants

PART A *Complete the following table.*

	SOURCE	SINK
Definition	a.	c.
Examples (plant parts)	b.	d.

1. Complete the table.

PART B *Answer the following questions on the lines provided.*

1. What causes the movement of sugars into phloem cells in leaves?

_____

_____

_____

_____

2. Where do the sugars that enter the phloem cells in leaves come from?

_____

_____

_____

_____

3. What causes the movement of water into phloem cells in leaves?

_____

_____

_____

_____

4. According to the pressure-flow hypothesis, what causes the flow of sugars from a source to a sink?

_____

_____

_____

Worksheet 34

Angiosperm Reproduction

▪ ▪

PART A *Use the diagram to answer the following.*

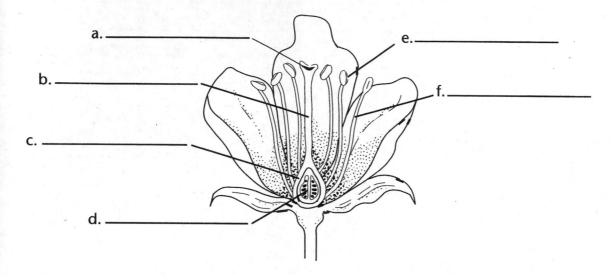

a. _____

b. _____

c. _____

d. _____

e. _____

f. _____

1. Label the plant's reproductive parts by writing one of the following terms in each of the spaces provided: filament, ovary, style, ovule, stigma, anther.

2. Which of the parts listed above make up the pistil?

_____

_____

_____

3. Which of the parts listed above make up the stamen?

_____

_____

_____

4. In which of the parts listed above are pollen grains formed?

_____

_____

_____

5. After fertilization, which of the parts listed above will become the seed?

_____

_____

_____

PART B *Complete the description of angiosperm reproduction by filling in each blank with one of the following terms: fertilization, mitosis, pollination, or meiosis.*

1. Sexual reproduction begins when microspores form by _____ in the anthers.

2. Each of the microspores undergoes _____ to form a pollen grain.

3. At the same time, megaspores form in the ovule by _____ .

4. One megaspore in each ovule undergoes _____ to form an egg.

5. _____ occurs when a pollen grain lands on a receptive stigma.

6. A pollen tube grows delivering sperm nuclei to the ovule, where _____ occurs.

7. In the process called double _____, one sperm fertilizes the egg and another sperm fertilizes two polar bodies.

8. The egg and sperm combine to form a zygote, which undergoes _____ to become the plant embryo.

Worksheet 35

Earthworm Anatomy

▪ ▪

PART A *Match each term with its corresponding structure in the diagram by writing the correct letter on the lines provided.*

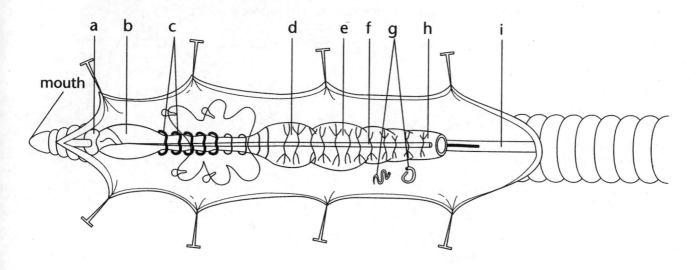

1. _____ gizzard

2. _____ brain

3. _____ nephridia

4. _____ aortic arches

5. _____ nerve cord

6. _____ intestine

7. _____ pharynx

8. _____ blood vessel

9. _____ crop

PART B *Match each structure with its description by writing the correct letter on the lines provided.*

1. _____ smooth area, a third of the way back from the head

2. _____ bristles used in locomotion

3. _____ fluid-filled body cavity

4. _____ opening for expelling waste

5. _____ excretory organ

6. _____ pumps blood through the open circulatory system

7. _____ acts as a pump to suck up food

8. _____ grinds up food

9. _____ completes digestion of food

10. _____ thin outer layer

a. coelom

b. aortic arch

c. gizzard

d. intestine

e. cuticle

f. clitellum

g. pharynx

h. nephridium

i. setae

j. nephridopore

Worksheet 36

Crayfish Anatomy

▪ ▪

PART A *Match each term with its corresponding structure in the diagram by writing the correct letter on the lines provided.*

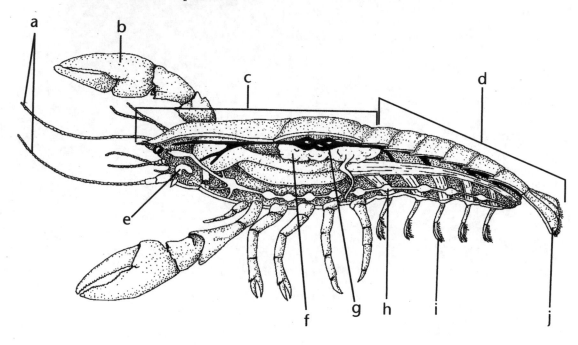

1. _____ abdomen

2. _____ heart

3. _____ green gland

4. _____ pinching legs

5. _____ telson

6. _____ nerve cord

7. _____ antennae

8. _____ gonad

9. _____ swimmeret

10. _____ cephalothorax

PART B *Match each structure with its description by writing the correct letter on the lines provided.*

1. _____ outer exoskeletal covering

2. _____ organ that regulates salt and water levels in blood

3. _____ body region that includes the head and thorax

4. _____ movable sensory structures

5. _____ respiratory organs attached to the walking legs

6. _____ pumps blood through the open circulatory system

7. _____ gamete-producing structures located directly beneath the heart

8. _____ mouth parts that chew and crush food

9. _____ paired fin on the abdomen that allows rapid backward movement

10. _____ legs specialized for swimming

a. heart

b. testes or ovaries

c. gills

d. telson

e. mandibles

f. cephalothorax

g. antennae

h. carapace

i. swimmerets

j. green gland

Worksheet 37

Frog Anatomy

■ ■

PART A *Use the diagram to answer the following questions.*

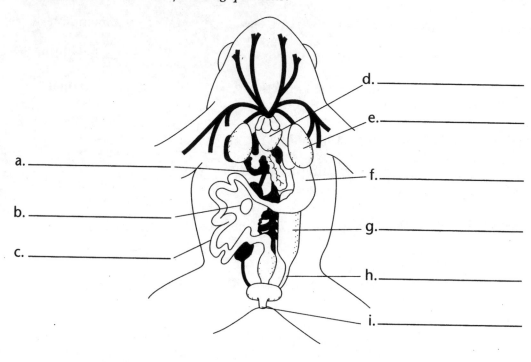

d. _____

e. _____

a. _____

f. _____

b. _____

g. _____

c. _____

h. _____

i. _____

1. Label the following structures in the spaces provided: cloaca, spleen, heart, kidney, small intestine, liver, ureter, stomach, lung.

2. Which of the labeled structures are part of the circulatory system?

_____

_____

_____

3. Which of the labeled structures are part of the digestive system?

_____

_____

_____

4. Which of the labeled structures are part of the excretory system?

_____

_____

_____

PART B *Answer the following.*

1. Describe the frog's respiratory system.

   _____

   _____

   _____

   _____

   _____

2. Describe the location and structure of the frog's heart.

   _____

   _____

   _____

   _____

   _____

3. Describe the functions and location of the cloaca.

   _____

   _____

   _____

   _____

   _____

4. Describe the function and location of the frog's skeletal muscles.

   _____

   _____

   _____

   _____

   _____

Worksheet 38

Muscle Contraction

• •

PART A *Using the diagram below, match each letter with the correct term by writing a letter in each space provided. Some letters will be used more than once.*

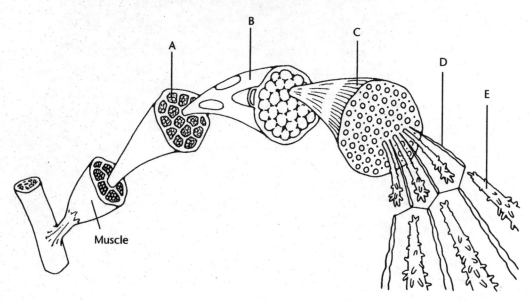

Muscle

1. _____ actin

2. _____ myofibril

3. _____ muscle fiber

4. _____ thick filament

5. _____ thin filament

6. _____ muscle bundle

7. _____ mysosin

8. _____ individual muscle cell

PART B *Answer the following.*

	DURING MUSCLE CONTRACTION	DURING MUSCLE RELAXATION
How does sarcomere shape change?	a.	c.
How does the distance between Z lines change?	b.	d.

1. Complete the table.

2. Explain why the accepted theory of how skeletal muscles move is called the "sliding filament" theory.

_____

_____

_____

_____

_____

3. Describe the role of ATP in muscle contraction.

_____

_____

_____

_____

Worksheet 39

Human Digestion

■ ■

PART A *Answer the following questions on the lines provided.*

1. What is mechanical digestion and where does it begin?

_____

_____

_____

2. What is chemical digestion and where does it begin?

_____

_____

_____

3. Complete the table.

	Type of Nutrient		
	CARBOHYDRATES	**FATS**	**PROTEINS**
Where is digestion of this nutrient completed?	a.	d.	g.
What are the final break down products of this nutrient?	b.	e.	h.
Do the breakdown products enter the blood or the lymph?	c.	f.	i.

PART B *Describe the role of each structure in digestion.*

1. Teeth

_____

_____

_____

2. Salivary glands

_____

_____

_____

3. Esophagus

_____

_____

_____

4. Stomach

_____

_____

_____

5. Liver

_____

_____

_____

6. Small intestine

_____

_____

_____

7. Pancreas

_____

_____

_____

Worksheet 40

Kidney Function

- -

PART A *Complete the following tables.*

STRUCTURE	FUNCTION
Kidney	1.
Renal artery	2.
Renal vein	3.
Bowman's capsule	4.
Glomerulus	5.

PROCESS	DESCRIPTION
Filtration	6.
Reabsorption	7.
Secretion	8.

PART B *Answer the following questions on the lines provided.*

1. Based on your knowledge kidney function, where would you expect the concentration of urea to be greater, in the renal artery or the renal veins? Explain your answer.

   _____

   _____

   _____

2. Describe what will happen to each of the following substances after they are carried by the blood to a glomerulus.

   a. Proteins

   _____

   _____

   b. Amino acids

   _____

   _____

   c. Urea

   _____

   _____

   d. Glucose

   _____

   _____

Worksheet 41

Human Respiration

- -

PART A *Answer the following questions on the lines provided.*

1. Explain how the volume of your chest cavity changes as you breathe.

_____

_____

2. What muscles are responsible for these changes in chest cavity volume?

_____

3. What is the normal resting respiratory rate (number of breaths per minute)?

_____

4. Describe each of the structures that inhaled air must pass through on the way to the alveoli.

_____

_____

_____

PART B *Use the diagram to answer the following questions.*

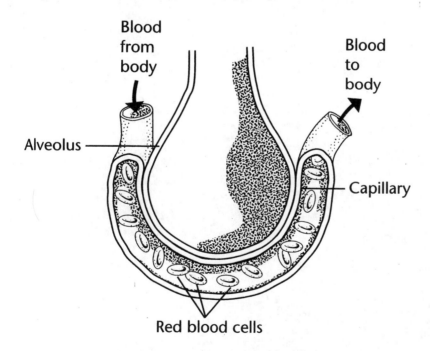

1. Complete the diagram by drawing and labeling two arrows, one showing the direction of oxygen movement, the other showing the direction of carbon dioxide movement.

2. What fills the space inside an alveolus?

_____

_____

3. How many alveoli are in your lungs?

_____

_____

Worksheet 42

Circulatory Systems

- -

PART A *Answer the following questions on the lines provided.*

1. What is the function of a circulatory system?

_____

_____

_____

_____

2. How are open and closed circulatory systems similar?

_____

_____

_____

_____

_____

3. How do open and closed circulatory systems differ?

_____

_____

_____

_____

_____

_____

PART B *Indicate whether each of the organisms listed below has an open or closed circulatory system by writing either* O *or* C *on the lines provided.*

1. _____ frog   **6.** _____ crab

2. _____ shark   **7.** _____ eagle

3. _____ beetle   **8.** _____ tarantula

4. _____ kangaroo   **9.** _____ earthworm

5. _____ human   **10.** _____ snail

Worksheet 43

Human Circulation

. . . . .

PART A *Use the diagram of human blood circulation to answer the following questions.*

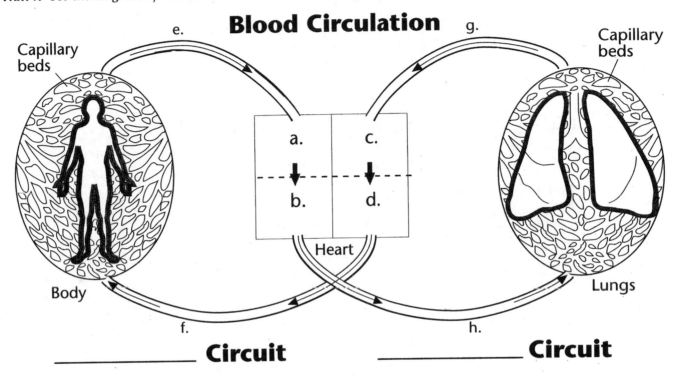

Blood Circulation

Capillary beds

Body

Heart

Lungs

Capillary beds

_____ **Circuit**

_____ **Circuit**

1. Label the systemic and pulmonary circuits by writing in the blanks provided.

2. Identify which chamber of the heart each letter corresponds to.

    a. _____

    b. _____

    c. _____

    d. _____

3. Which of the labeled vessels are arteries?

_____

4. Which of the labeled vessels are veins?

_____

5. Which of the labeled vessels carry oxygenated blood?

_____

6. Which of the labeled vessels carry deoxygenated blood?

_____

PART B *Match each description with its structure by writing the correct letter on the lines provided.*

1. _____ Thick-walled chamber that pumps out well-oxygenated blood.

2. _____ Thick-walled chamber that pumps out oxygen-poor blood.

3. _____ Thin-walled chamber that receives oxygen-poor blood from the body.

4. _____ Thin-walled chamber that receives oxygen-rich blood from the lungs.

5. _____ Chamber that receives blood from the left atrium.

6. _____ Chamber that receives blood from the right atrium.

7. _____ Chamber that pumps blood into the left ventricle.

8. _____ Chamber that pumps blood into the right ventricle.

9. _____ Chamber that pumps blood into the pulmonary arteries.

10. _____ Chamber that receives blood from the pulmonary veins.

a. right atrium

b. left atrium

c. right ventricle

d. left ventricle

Worksheet 44

Inflammatory Response

PART A *Explain the underlying cause of each of these symptoms of inflammation.*

1. Swelling

_____

_____

_____

2. Redness

_____

_____

_____

3. Warmth

_____

_____

_____

PART B *Answer the following questions on the lines provided.*

1. Describe the role of white blood cells in the inflammatory response. What brings them to the inflamed area and what do they do when they arrive?

_____

_____

_____

_____

2. The release of histamine by injured tissue is the primary signal to the body to start the inflammatory response. The drug aspirin slows histamine release. Explain the possible advantages and disadvantages of taking aspirin after an injury.

_____

_____

_____

_____

Worksheet 45

Humoral Immunity

- -

PART A *Draw an antibody molecule in the space below. Indicate where the antigen-binding sites are located.*

PART B *Answer the following on the lines provided.*

1. What is a pathogen?

_____

_____

_____

2. What is an antigen?

_____

_____

_____

_____

3. Describe how antibodies protect your body against disease when exposed to a virus.

_____

_____

_____

_____

Worksheet 46

Cell-Mediated Immunity

PART A *Complete the table.*

CELL TYPE	ROLL IN CELL-MEDIATED IMMUNITY
Macrophage	1.
Killer T Cell	2.
Helper T Cell	3.
Suppressor T Cell	4.

PART B *The steps in cell mediated immunity are described below. Place them in sequential order by writing a number on the blank line beside each description.*

a. _____ A helper T cell recognizes the antigen on the surface of the macrophage and binds to the macrophage-antigen complex.

b. _____ The macrophage sends a chemical message to helper T cells, stimulating them to divide.

c. _____ When the antigens are no longer present, suppressor T cells turn off the immune response.

d. _____ Helper T cells secrete a substance that activates killer T cells.

e. _____ Killer T cells release perforin, which makes holes in the surface of infected cells, destroying them.

f. _____ A macrophage engulfs a pathogen, destroys it, and displays pieces of antigen on its surface.

g. _____ Activated killer T cells recognize an antigen on the surface of infected cells and bind to it.

Worksheet 47

Regulation of Blood Sugar

▪ ▪

PART A *Complete the table.*

	PANCREATIC HORMONE	
	GLUCAGON	**INSULIN**
Which pancreatic cells secrete this hormone?	a.	d.
What triggers its secretion?	b.	e.
What effect does it have on the level of sugar in the blood?	c.	f.

PART B *Answer the following questions on the lines provided.*

1. What pancreatic hormone would you expect to find at high levels in the blood of someone who has just eaten a large meal?

_____

_____

2. What pancreatic hormone would you expect to find at high levels in the blood of someone who has just completed a 10 kilometer run?

_____

_____

3. Describe how the body's regulation of blood sugar is like the regulation of a house's temperature by a heating system with a thermostat.

_____

_____

_____

_____

_____

Worksheet 48

Action Potential

. . . . .

PART A *Use the diagram to answer the questions below.*

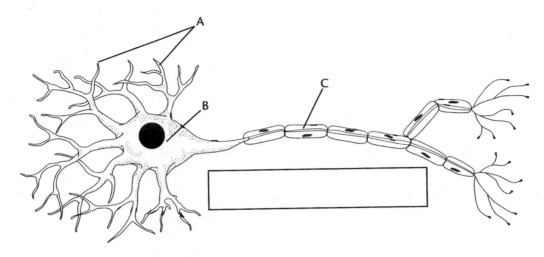

1. Identify the labeled parts of the neuron.

a. _____

b. _____

c. _____

2. Draw an arrow in the rectangular box above to indicate the direction in which the neural impulse flows.

3. Assume the section of neuron labeled as C is in its resting state. Describe what this means in terms of the charge difference between the inner and outer surface of the neuron.

_____

_____

_____

_____

_____

PART B *Answer the following questions on the lines provided.*

1. Describe the sequence in which the ion channels open during an action potential.

_____

_____

_____

_____

_____

_____

2. What effect does the opening of the sodium channels have on the charge difference across the neuron's membrane?

_____

_____

_____

_____

3. What effect does the opening of the potassium channels have on the charge difference across the neuron's membrane?

_____

_____

_____

_____

4. Explain what makes a nerve impulse travel along an axon.

_____

_____

_____

_____

_____

Worksheet 49

Synaptic Transmission

PART A *Use the diagram to answer the questions below*

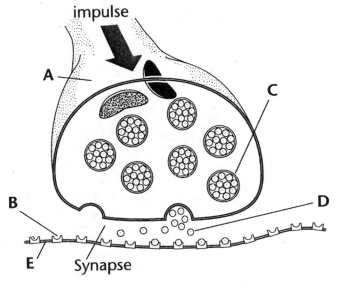

impulse

A

C

B   D

E   Synapse

1. If this was a synapse between a motor neuron and a muscle, which of the letters would represent the muscle cell?

_____

2. Which letter would designate the axon of the motor neuron?

_____

3. What is inside the structure labeled C?

_____

4. Which of the labeled structures represents a receptor site?

_____

PART B *In the space below, draw a diagram that shows what happens when a nerve impulse arrives at a synapse.*

Answer Key
■ ■

Worksheet 1

PART A
1. a. Two or more elements combined chemically.
   b. A substance that cannot by broken down by chemical processes into simpler substances.
   c. Answers will vary, but include carbon dioxide.
   d. Answers will vary, but include carbon and oxygen.

PART B
1. b
2. a
3. c
4. a
5. a
6. b and c

Worksheet 2

PART A
1. An atom that has lost or gained electrons.
2. Forces that hold two or more atoms together.

PART B
1. a. 2
   b. 8
   c. 8
   d. 2
   e. 8
   f. 7
   g. 2
   h. 8
   i. 1
2. The outer shell of chlorine can hold eight electrons, but it holds only seven. The outer shell of sodium can hold eight electrons, but it holds only one. If sodium gives up its one electron to chlorine, the outer shells of both ions will be filled.

Worksheet 3

PART A
1. Oxygen should have eight electrons; two at lowest energy level and six at outer level. Hydrogen should have one electron.

PART B
1. The outer energy level can hold eight electrons, but there are only six present. The outer energy level of the hydrogen atom can hold two electrons, but only one is present. If oxygen bonds to two hydrogen atoms all the atoms will have their outer energy levels filled.
2. Single bonds involve sharing one pair of electrons, double bonds involve sharing two pairs of electrons and triple bonds involve sharing three pairs of electrons.

Worksheet 4

PART A
1. to speed up a chemical reaction
2. proteins
3. the enzyme
4. The bonds weaken.
5. The active site of an enzyme is specific to the substrate. If the enzyme is misshapen, the substrate may not bind correctly to the active site.

PART B
1. c
2. d
3. e
4. a
5. b

Worksheet 5

PART A
1. net movement of molecules from an area of high concentration to an area of low concentration
2. a membrane that allows only certain molecules to pass through
3. the diffusion of water across a semipermeable membrane

PART B
1. a. Cell is unaffected.
   b. Cell shrinks.
   c. Cell swells and bursts.
2. The solute concentration is greater in a *Paramecium* than in its environment.
3. There would no longer be a net movement of water into the *Paramecium*.

Worksheet 6

PART A
1. a. yes
   b. no
   c. no
2. a. yes
   b. no
   c. no
3. a. yes
   b. yes
   c. no
4. a. yes
   b. no
   c. no

PART B

1. Possible answers include oxygen, water, carbon dioxide, and amino acids.
2. Possible answers include proteins and carbohydrates.
3. Charged particles cannot move through the layer of lipid tails in the membrane.
4. Both move molecules down their concentration gradients.
5. Facilitated transport uses a carrier protein; diffusion does not.
6. Both use carrier proteins.
7. Facilitated transport doesn't require energy input; active transport does. Facilitated transport moves substances down concentration gradients; active transport moves substances against gradients.
8. ATP energy is used to change the shape of a carrier molecule so that it moves sodium ions out of the cell. The protein then changes shape again and moves potassium ions into the cell.

Worksheet 7

PART A

1. a process by which wastes and cell products are secreted out of a cell through the cell membrane
2. a form of active transport in which a portion of the cell membrane surrounds outside particles and moves them into the cell
3. a form of endocytosis; the process by which a cell engulfs a food particle or other solid substance

PART B

1. Both processes involve the bulk movement of substances across the cell membrane by means of a vesicle.
2. Endocytosis moves things into the cell; exocytosis moves them out.
3. a membrane-bound sac
4. They engulf bacteria and other substances.
5. phagocytosis or endocytosis
6. A vesicle filled with digestive enzymes. It is used to break down or digest things.
7. waste material or cell products to be secreted

Worksheet 8

PART A

1. a. three phosphates
   b. adenine
   c. ribose
2. adenosine triphosphate
3. ribose
4. ATP has three phosphates; ADP has two.
5. ATP is "charged up" by energy from food, just as a battery is charged by a power source. Then the energy in ATP is used to power cellular processes, just as a battery is used to run a flashlight or other device.

PART B

1. Answers will vary. Diagram should include the fact that energy is required to bind ADP and phosphate to form ATP. Energy is released when ATP breaks its bond with a phosphate to form ADP and phosphate. This cycle repeats.

Worksheet 9

PART A

1. The process by which some organisms convert sunlight to a usable form of energy.
2. carbohydrates

PART B

1. a. H_2O
   b. O_2
   c. and d. ATP and NADPH
   e. CO_2
   f. carbohydrates
2. They take it in from the air.

Worksheet 10

PART A

1. d
2. b
3. a
4. c
5. e

PART B

1. Light is used by the two photosystems. Photosystem II uses light energy to split water. Photosystem I uses light energy to re-energize electrons transferred from photosystem II.
2. Photosystems I and II are embedded in the membrane of the thylakoids.
3. ATP and NADPH

Worksheet 11

PART A

1. chloroplast
2. a. thylakoid
   b. stroma
3. "Stroma" should be circled.

PART B

1. a. RuBP
   b. PGA
   c. ATP
   d. NADPH
   e. RuBP
   f. ATP

Worksheet 12

PART A

1. glucose, oxygen
2. water, carbon dioxide, ATP

PART B

1. a
2. a
3. b
4. c
5. b and c
6. a
7. b

Worksheet 13
PART A
1. glucose
2. 6
3. pyruvate
4. 3
5. ATP
6. from food
PART B
1. a. glucose
   b. ATP
   c. ADP
   d. ADP
   e. ATP
   f. NADH
   g. pyruvate

Worksheet 14
PART A
1. One of the carbons is expelled as carbon dioxide. The other two become attached to coenzyme A to form acetyl-CoA.
2. NADH, ATP, $FADH_2$
3. Citric acid is formed when acetyl-CoA is linked to a 4-carbon compound.
4. They are released as carbon dioxide.
5. The 4-carbon compound that acetyl-CoA combined with to start the reactions is regenerated and used over and over.
6. They are used to power the final stage of aerobic respiration, the electron transport chain.
7. They are exhaled.
PART B
1. mitochondrion
2. a. outer membrane
   b. matrix
   c. inner membrane
3. "Matrix" should be circled.

Worksheet 15
PART A
1. mitochondrion
2. NAD+
3. It is made of protein and is embedded in the inner mitochondrial membrane.
4. Hydrogen ions are pumped from the mitochondrial matrix into the outer compartment.
5. It decreases.
6. oxygen
7. Hydrogen ions flow down their concentration gradient, through ATP synthase, which converts ADP to ATP.
8. Water is formed when the electrons combine with oxygen in the final step.
PART B
1. a. outer mitochondrial compartment
   b. inner mitochondrial membrane
   c. mitochondrial matrix
   d. first electron carrier protein
   e. ATP synthase

Worksheet 16
PART A
1. a. interphase
   b. prophase
   c. metaphase
   d. anaphase
   e. telophase
2. "Interphase" should be circled.
PART B
1. e
2. d
3. c
4. b
5. a

Worksheet 17
PART A
1. a matching pair of chromosomes, one from the father and one from the mother
2. two identical copies of each chromosome attached by a centromere
3. anaphase I
4. anaphase II
5. Sister chromatids (before crossing over) are identical. Homologous chromosomes carry different alleles.
6. A diploid cell contains two of each type of chromosome. A haploid cell contains one of each type.
7. 48
8. 7
9. haploid
10. diploid
PART B
1. Products of meiosis I should be two cells, each with one black and one white duplicated chromosome. Products of meiosis II should be four cells, each with one black and one white unduplicated chromosome.

Worksheet 18
PART A
1. d
2. g
3. c
4. h
5. b
6. e
7. a
8. f
PART B
1. c
2. d
3. a, c
4. b, d, e, f
5. b
6. f

Worksheet 19
PART A
1. unit of hereditary material that determines a particular trait of an organism
2. one form of a gene for a particular trait
3. a cell that contains two matching sets of chromosomes, one inherited from each parent
PART B
1. They are the same size and shape, and they carry genes for the same traits. They differ in that they carry different alleles.
2. The members of each homologous pair are separated and moved to opposite ends of the cell.
3. When the homologous chromosomes are separated, the alleles they carry also separate.
4. As a result of the segregation of chromosomes during meiosis, each sperm or egg cell receives a different set of alleles.

Worksheet 20
PART A
1. Mice live.
2. Mice die.
3. Mice live.
4. Mice die.
PART B
1. The S bacteria's deadliness is a result of its mucous coat.
2. He heated the bacteria to kill them without destroying their coats, then injected the dead bacteria into mice.
3. No.
4. The bacteria that had been changed from R to S gave rise to new S bacteria.

Worksheet 21
PART A
1. a and d
2. b and c
3. adenine
4. thymine
5. hydrogen bonds
6. covalent bonds
PART B
1. The hydrogen bonds between the two strands are broken, and the DNA is unwound.
2. DNA polymerase
3. The strands face in opposite directions, but DNA polymerase can work in only one direction.
4. sugars and phosphates
5. nitrogenous bases
6. a. thymine
   b. cytosine
   c. adenine
   d. guanine
   e. adenine
   f. guanine
   g. thymine
   h. cytosine

Worksheet 22
PART A
1. 2
2. 3
3. 3 and 4
4. prophase I
PART B
1. a. AB or ab
   b. AB or ab
   c. aB or Ab
   d. aB or Ab

Worksheet 23
PART A
1. a. Drawing should show one large X and one smaller Y chromosome.
   b. Drawing should show two sperm, one carrying X, the other carrying Y.
   c. Drawing should show two large X chromosomes.
   d. Drawing should show egg with X chromosome.
PART B
1. 22
2. 22
3. The father's. All eggs carry an X chromosome. The sperm can provide either an X or a Y chromosome, thus determining the offspring's sex.

Worksheet 24
PART A
1. Drawing A should show one cell with a single chromatid, the other with a single chromatid and a homologous pair. In drawing B, each cell should contain one black and one white chromatid.
PART B
1. It increases chromosome number in one gamete and decreases it in the other.
2. Nondisjunction of chromosome 21 occurred when one of the parental gametes was forming. When this gamete with two copies of chromosome 21 combined with a normal gamete at fertilization, the zygote received three copies of this chromosome.

Worksheet 25
PART A
1. cytosine
2. uracil
3. adenine
4. guanine
PART B
1. RNA contains uracil, DNA contains thymine. RNA contains ribose, DNA contains deoxyribose. RNA is single-stranded, DNA is usually double-stranded.
2. in the nucleus
3. The DNA is unwound.
4. RNA polymerase
5. messenger RNA

Worksheet 26

PART A
1. b
2. d
3. e
4. c
5. a
6. g
7. f

PART B
1. a. CGU
   b. AAA
   c. UGG
2. tRNAs bind to complementary RNA codons and deliver their attached amino acids to the correct place in the growing amino acid chain.

Worksheet 27/28

PART A
1. the process by which a chromosome breaks off and is incorporated into its homologous chromosome, giving that chromosome an extra copy of a DNA sequence
2. the process by which a chromosome breaks and a segment of DNA is lost
3. the process by which a chromosome breaks off, turns around, and reattaches itself in the reverse order to the same chromosome
4. the process by which a chromosome breaks off and attaches to a different, nonhomologous chromosome

PART B
1. a. deletion
   b. inversion
   c. deletion
   d. translocation
   e. duplication
   f. inversion
   g. duplication
2. A deletion is the most harmful, because a gene that takes part in some vital process can be lost. Having an extra copy of a gene or a reversed copy or having the gene present on a different chromosome is less harmful.
3. Both duplication and translocation can add genes to a chromosome. In duplication, the extra genes are additional copies of genes already present. In translocation, the extra genes are from a nonhomologous chromosome.
4. Duplication occurs more frequently, because homologous chromosomes are more closely aligned during prophase I than are nonhomologous chromosomes.
5. prophase I
6. inversion

Worksheet 29

PART A
1. translation
2. transcription

PART B
1. 2
2. 4
3. lysine
4. a. no
   b. yes
   c. no
   d. no
   e. yes
   f. yes

Worksheet 30

PART A
1. the single-stranded ends of a fragment of double-stranded DNA that are available to bind to complementary bases of another "sticky end"
2. a circle of DNA that is separate from the main bacterial chromosome
3. an enzyme used to join the phosphate/sugar backbones of two pieces of DNA

PART B
1. It is cut into pieces by a special enzyme.
2. It is cut with the same enzyme that the human DNA was cut with.
3. The complementary bases of the cut "sticky ends" pair up.
4. Some bacteria contain a plasmid that makes them resistant to tetracycline.
5. If the human insulin gene is successfully transferred, it cuts the bacterial gene for tetracycline resistance. Thus, scientists know that those bacteria that cannot grow on tetracycline contain the human insulin gene.

Worksheet 31

PART A
1. a. A virus attaches to the host cell.
   b. The virus injects its DNA.
   c. The viral DNA instructs the host to produce viral proteins and DNA.
   d. The DNA and proteins assemble to form new viruses.
   e. The host cell lyses, releasing the new viruses.

PART B
1. c
2. In the lysogenic cycle, the virus does not immediately kill the host. Instead the viral DNA becomes an inactive prophage that is passed on to the cells' descendants. In the lytic cycle, the virus seizes control of the host cell, uses it to make new viruses, and kills the host when the viruses are released.
3. viral DNA integrated into the host's DNA; during the lysogenic cycle
4. the cell that a virus infects
5. A cell that is in the lysogenic cycle will enter the lytic cycle if the prophage breaks free from the cell's DNA.

Worksheet 32

PART A
1. Evaporation of water from plant parts.
2. The vascular tissue that carries water and dissolved minerals upward in a plant.

PART B

1. They can close their pores.
2. carbon dioxide
3. It reduces water evaporation.
4. xylem
5. the evaporation of water from leaves (transpiration)
6. cohesion of the molecules

Worksheet 33

PART A

1. a. Area where sugars are produced by photosynthesis.
   b. leaves
   c. Area where sugars are used.
   d. growing tips and roots

PART B

1. Sugars are actively transported into phloem cells.
2. They are produced by photosynthesis.
3. osmosis
4. The pressure difference between the two areas. Pressure is high at sources and lower at sinks.

Worksheet 34

PART A

1. a. stigma
   b. style
   c. ovary
   d. ovule
   e. anther
   f. filament
2. stigma, style and ovary
3. anther and filament
4. anther
5. ovule

PART B

1. meiosis
2. mitosis
3. meiosis
4. mitosis
5. pollination
6. fertilization
7. fertilization
8. mitosis

Worksheet 35

PART A

1. e
2. a
3. g
4. c
5. i
6. h
7. b
8. f
9. d

PART B

1. f
2. i
3. a
4. j
5. h
6. b
7. g
8. c
9. d
10. e

Worksheet 36

PART A

1. d
2. g
3. e
4. b
5. j
6. h
7. a
8. f
9. i
10. c

PART B

1. h
2. j
3. f
4. g
5. c
6. a
7. b
8. e
9. d
10. i

Worksheet 37

PART A

1. a. liver
   b. spleen
   c. small intestine
   d. heart
   e. lung
   f. stomach
   g. kidney
   h. ureter
   i. cloaca
2. heart, spleen
3. stomach, small intestine, cloaca, liver (accessory structure)
4. kidney, ureter, cloaca

PART B

1. The frog breathes air and has lungs, but also carries out some gas exchange through its skin.
2. The frog's heart is in the center of its chest between the lungs. It consists of three chambers—two atria and one ventricle.
3. The cloaca is located between the frog's hind legs. Gametes and waste from the urinary and excretory systems leave the body through the cloaca.
4. The frog's skeletal muscles are found just beneath the skin. They pull on bones to allow the frog to move.

Worksheet 38

PART A
1. d
2. c
3. b
4. e
5. d
6. a
7. e
8. b

PART B
1. a. sarcomere shortens
   b. distance decreases
   c. sarcomere lengthens
   d. distance increases
2. According to this theory, muscle contraction occurs when the thin filaments slide past the thick filaments, shortening the muscle.
3. ATP binds to myosin. The breakdown of this ATP allows the cross bridges between the actin and myosin to bend, pulling the actin past the myosin and causing the muscle to contract.

Worksheet 39

PART A
1. The mechanical breaking of food into smaller pieces. It begins in the mouth.
2. The chemical breakdown of food into simpler molecules. It begins in the mouth.
3. a. small intestine
   b. monosaccharides
   c. blood
   d. small intestine
   e. fatty acids and glycerol
   f. lymph
   g. small intestine
   h. amino acids
   i. blood

PART B
1. Help break food into smaller pieces.
2. Secrete enzyme-containing saliva.
3. Moves chewed food to the stomach.
4. Mixes and churns food that is swallowed.
5. Secretes bile which is used in fat digestion.
6. The major site of food digestion and absorption.
7. Secretes a variety of digestive enzymes into the small intestine.

Worksheet 40

PART A
1. Removes wastes from the blood.
2. Delivers blood to the kidney.
3. Moves blood away from the kidney.
4. Collects filtrate from the glomerulus.
5. Acts as a filter through which some substances from the blood may pass.
6. The movement of small molecules from the glomerulus into the Bowman's capsule.
7. The return of molecules from the renal tubule to the blood.
8. The movement of substances to be secreted from the blood into the renal tubule.

PART B
1. Urea concentration will be higher in the renal arteries. Urea is removed from the blood as it travels through the kidney before exiting via the renal vein.
2. a. Proteins remain in the blood.
   b. Amino acids enter the renal tubule during filtration, then are reabsorbed into the bloodstream.
   c. Urea enters the renal tubule during filtration and is excreted in the urine.
   d. Glucose enters the renal tubule during filtration, then is reabsorbed into the bloodstream.

Worksheet 41

PART A
1. It increases with inhalation and decreases with exhalation.
2. diaphragm and intercostal muscles
3. 12-15 breaths per minute
4. To reach an alveolus, air must enter through the nose or mouth, then pass through the pharynx or throat, the larynx, the trachea, a bronchus, and a bronchiole.

PART B
1. Arrow labeled carbon dioxide should point from the red blood cells into the alveolus. Arrow labeled oxygen should point from the alveolus into a red blood cell.
2. air
3. millions

Worksheet 42

PART A
1. To distribute oxygen and nutrients to cells, and to remove carbon dioxide and other wastes from the body.
2. Both include at least one heart and a system of vessels.
3. In an open circulatory system the blood flows among the body tissues. In a closed circulatory system the blood is always confined to vessels.

PART B
1. C
2. C
3. O
4. C
5. C
6. O
7. C
8. O
9. C
10. O

Worksheet 43

PART A

1. Systemic at left, pulmonary at right.
2. a. right atrium
   b. right ventricle
   c. left atrium
   d. left ventricle
3. f and h
4. e and g
5. f and g
6. e and h

PART B

1. d
2. c
3. a
4. b
5. d
6. c
7. b
8. a
9. c
10. b

Worksheet 44

PART A

1. Plasma fluid escapes from the blood vessels into the tissues, causing them to swell.
2. Blood vessels expand, bringing more blood to the area.
3. Increased blood flow also heats the area.

PART B

1. White blood cells are attracted to the injured area by chemical signals released by the injured tissue. They squeeze out through the walls of the blood vessels and engulf and digest pathogens and damaged tissue.
2. The advantage would be that the injured area would not swell as much and so would be less painful. The disadvantage would be that the recruitment of white blood cells to the area would also be lessened.

Worksheet 45

PART A

1. Drawing should be of a Y-shaped molecule, with the tips of the arms labeled as antigen-binding sites.

PART B

1. a disease-causing organism or virus
2. a molecule that the body's immune system responds to
3. Antibodies bind to specific antigens on the virus and to one another, forming virus-antibody clumps. This inactivates the virus so that it cannot infect other cells.

Worksheet 46

PART A

1. engulf pathogens and break them down, display antigen, bind to and activate helper T cells
2. bind to infected cells and destroy them
3. stimulate the production of killer T cells
4. turn off the production of killer T cells

PART B

1. a. 2
   b. 3
   c. 7
   d. 4
   e. 6
   f. 1
   g. 5

Worksheet 47

PART A

1. a. alpha cells
   b. a fall in blood glucose level
   c. increases it
   d. beta cells
   e. a rise in blood glucose level
   f. decreases it

PART B

1. insulin
2. glucagon
3. Both are examples of negative feedback systems. Low temperature turns on a heating system which raises the temperature, and then turns off the heat. Similarly high blood sugar turns on insulin secretion which lowers the blood sugar level, and then turns off insulin secretion.

Worksheet 48

PART A

1. a. dendrites
   b. cell body
   c. axon
2. Arrow should point to the right.
3. The inner surface of the nerve cell membrane has a more negative charge, and the outer surface has a more positive charge.

PART B

1. Sodium channels open first. Potassium channels open second.
2. It reverses the charge across the membrane, making the inside more positive than the outside.
3. It restores the cell to its resting potential.
4. The reversal of charge in one area of the membrane triggers the opening of sodium channels in the adjacent area of the membrane. This sequential opening of adjacent sodium gates moves the impulse along the axon.

Worksheet 49

PART A

1. e
2. a
3. neurotransmitters (chemical messengers)
4. b

PART B

Drawings should show the flow of neurotransmitters across the synapse, causing a change in the membrane potential of the next neuron or effector cell.